MEETING THE GOVERNING CHALLENGE

Applying the High-Impact Governing Model in Your Organization

By

Doug Eadie

President & CEO
Doug Eadie & Company

A Governance Edge®Publication

A publication of
Governance Edge®
Doug Eadie & Company
3 Sunny Point Terrace
Oldsmar, FL 34677

Phone: 800-209-7652
Email: info@GovernanceEdge.com
A complete listing of books and CDs by Doug Eadie is available at www.DougEadie.com.

ISBN 978-0-9798894-0-0
Library of Congress Control Number: 2007906291

Library of Congress Subject Headings:
Nonprofit organizations–Management
Boards of directors

TO MY WIFE

BARBARA CARLSON KRAI

TABLE OF CONTENTS

FOREWORD

The estimated fifteen to twenty million volunteers who serve on nonprofit boards in this country are truly a precious national asset. They bring dedication, commitment, knowledge, expertise, and community networks to the immensely important task of governing some 1 ½ million nonprofits engaged in aging, social services, health, education, transportation, community and economic development, association management, and other areas. All Americans have a huge stake in these volunteers' effectively carrying out their governing responsibilities: providing their organizations with clear strategic directions and policies, ensuring that they possess the resources required to carry out their missions fully, monitoring programmatic and financial performance, and maintaining close ties with key stakeholders in their communities.

Doug Eadie's *Meeting the Governing Challenge* is a rich resource and indispensable how-to guidebook for the members of what Doug calls the "Strategic Governing Team": board members, CEOs, and senior executives who work with boards. There's nothing theoretical about this powerful little book, which is based on Doug's twenty-five years of experience in working with some 500 nonprofit and public organizations. Doug's High-Impact Governing Model, which is at the heart of *Meeting the Governing Challenge*, goes well beyond the old-fashioned notion of governing as merely "policy making." It describes the work of governing as a dynamic decision-making process that relies heavily on well-designed board structure. I am especially pleased that Doug rightly sees the CEO as not only a close partner with the board in governing, but also as the person primarily accountable for developing the board's capacity to do the kind of high-impact governing work that these challenging times demand.

You'll want to keep *Meeting the Governing Challenge* close at hand and refer to it often as you lead your nonprofit into the future as part of its Strategic Governing Team.

Linda Kloss, President & CEO
American Health Information Management Association
Chicago, Illinois

ACKNOWLEDGMENTS

Although I am the author of *Meeting the Governing Challenge*, I could not have written nearly as good a book without the creative collaboration of many others, and so I must share credit for whatever merits this book possesses.

Over the past twenty-five years, I have been privileged to work with hundreds of nonprofit and public board members, CEOs, and senior executives in organizations of all shapes and sizes. I am indebted to them for the real-life lessons they have taught me, which have helped to make this book a much richer, more powerful resource for nonprofit and public leaders who are committed to high-impact board-CEO partnerships.

I want to thank several leaders who read the manuscript and provided me with valuable suggestions for improvement: Patrick Bassett, president, National Association of Independent Schools; Stephen Bland, chief executive officer, Port Authority of Allegheny County; Skardon Bliss, executive director, Florida Council of Independent Schools; Pamela Boswell, vice president for program management and educational services, American Public Transportation Association; Janegale Boyd, president & CEO, Florida Association of Homes and Services for the Aging; Ronnie Bryant, president & CEO, Charlotte Regional Partnership and chair of the Board of Directors, International Economic Development Council; Sue Buchholtz, president & CEO, Pinellas Association for Retarded Citizens; Linda Carter, president & CEO, Community Foundation of Broward; Paul Dugan, superintendent, Washoe County School District; Jeffrey Finkle, president & CEO, the International Economic Development Council; Jane Gallucci, member, Pinellas County Board of Education and immediate past president, National School Boards Association; John Hedrick, president, Denton County Transportation Authority; Gilbert Holmes, president & CEO, IndyGo (Indianapolis Public Transportation Corporation); Paul Houston, executive director, American Association of School Administrators; Virginia Jacko, president & CEO, Miami Lighthouse for the Blind and Visually Impaired; Linda Kloss, president & CEO, American Health Information Management Association; Dennis Koons, president & CEO, Michigan Bankers Association; Gary LaBranche, president & CEO, Association Forum of Chicagoland; Katie Burnham Laverty, president & CEO, Society for Nonprofit Organizations; James McGuirk, executive director, Astor Home for Children; Gregory Maciag, president & CEO, ACORD; Steven Marcus, president & CEO, the Health Foundation of South Florida; William Millar, president & CEO, American Public Transportation Association; Lynne Morsen, senior program manager, American Public Transportation Association; Jill Muehrcke, editor, *Nonprofit World*, Society for Nonprofit Organizations; Ellie Paladine, chair, Public Relations/Grants Committee, Community Foundation of Pasco County; Bill Scott, executive director, Kentucky School Boards Association; Curt Selquist, chair of the Board of Directors, National Alliance for Health Information Technology; Paul Sharman, president & CEO, Institute of Management Accountants; Michael Townes, executive director, Hampton Roads Transit; Peter Varga, executive director, the Rapid (Interurban Transit Partnership); and Clayton Wilcox, superintendent, Pinellas County School District.

Thomas Berger, president & CEO of Thomas Berger Marketing, offered insightful editorial suggestions and oversaw production of *Meeting the Governing Challenge*. Angela Ashe and Cathy Ordiway, members of the Doug Eadie & Company team, provided valuable administrative support that enabled me to focus on my writing task with minimal distractions.

My children, Jennifer and William, drawing on their extensive leadership experience, read the manuscript with a critical eye and helped me sharpen key concepts.

And I could not possibly have written *Meeting the Governing Challenge* while running a demanding consulting business without the encouragement and support of my dear friend, close professional colleague, and wife, Barbara Carlson Krai.

Of course, I alone am responsible for any shortcomings this book might have.

Doug Eadie
Oldsmar, Florida
August 2007

1. THE HIGH-IMPACT GOVERNING MODEL IN A NUTSHELL

THE GOVERNING CHALLENGE

I first worked with a nonprofit board when, as a young man of twenty-eight, I was hired as deputy executive director of the Greater Erie Community Action Committee (GECAC) in Erie, Pennsylvania. One of my most important objectives during my first year on the job was to work closely with the executive director and board in implementing a new board standing committee structure and related governing processes. Two things hit me right in the face as I began to work with the GECAC board:

- First, the board was an impressive group of people who brought diverse experience and expertise, myriad connections in the community, and tremendous commitment to the GECAC boardroom. The board was without question a precious resource that GECAC could tap in carrying out its important mission, which included early childhood education, workforce development, and community organization.

- Second, the GECAC board wasn't coming close to realizing its tremendous promise as a governing body. It was immediately obvious to me that merely getting really talented, bright, and dedicated people in a room together wouldn't produce effective governing.

So early in my career, I learned a valuable lesson: If you want your nonprofit or public board to function effectively as a governing body—doing what I call "high-impact" governing work that makes a real difference—you've got to develop that board, consciously and systematically, as a governing organization. In addition to getting qualified and committed people on the board, you've got to pay close attention to the board's role, structure and key governing processes.

In Erie, I discovered my professional reason for being—my mission if you will: to help nonprofit and public board members, CEOs, and senior executives in building their boards' capacity to do truly high-impact governing. This is a passionate mission for me, not only because I thoroughly enjoy working with board members and executives in the governing arena, but also because the stakes are so high. Think about it. Nonprofit and public organizations make a tremendous contribution to our social and economic well-being, providing an amazing array of services in such areas as health care, aging, transportation, education, economic and community development, and more. Their effectiveness in providing these essential services is clearly impacted by how well their boards do in making important governing decisions, such as setting strategic goals, establishing annual objectives, and adopting the annual budget. Governing is, indeed, a high-stakes "business"!

This book is written explicitly for you: nonprofit and public board members, CEOs, and senior executives who work directly with these boards. My purpose is to provide you with detailed, practical guidance that you can put to immediate use in transforming your boards into higher-impact governing bodies. This is, then, a very practical, how-to guidebook, not an academic tour of the governance terrain. The key concepts and techniques for board capacity building that I've learned and tested over my twenty-five years in the field of nonprofit and public leadership make up my High-Impact Governing Model™. Think of the Model as a powerful tool kit that I'm sharing with you to help you build the kind of board and board-CEO partnership that your organization needs to thrive and grow in these challenging times.

THE MODEL IN ACTION

If you turn to the Appendix at the end of this chapter, you'll find four detailed vignettes that, drawing on real-life experience, illustrate my High-Impact Governing Model™ in action:

• **Golden Horizon Homes:** an aging services organization whose board and CEO re-designed the annual operational planning/budget preparation process, building in the kind of creative, proactive board involvement that turned a formerly passive-reactive governing body into a much more engaged group of board members who felt tremendous satisfaction and truly owned their operational planning and budget decisions.

• **ABC Association:** an international trade association whose new board governance committee, headed by the board chair and including the other board standing committee chairs and the CEO, took the lead in strengthening the board's self-management capacity. This included setting individual board member performance targets and standing committee goals and monitoring performance, thereby creating a kind of continuous improvement program for the Association's governance function.

• **Forward Transit:** the regional public transportation agency for a four-county area in the Southeastern U.S., whose general manager actively engaged her executive team in preparing for board standing committee meetings via monthly half-day team meetings that were spearheaded by "chief staff liaisons," executive team members responsible for the care and feeding of the standing committees, including developing agenda items and making sure committee chairs were well prepared to lead their meetings.

• **Pleasantville School District:** a large, rapidly growing school district whose board of education, working closely with the superintendent and senior administrators, successfully handled a highly complex, potentially controversial strategic issue—redrawing school boundaries—by involving the board in an intensive "strategic work session" at which the issue was identified, and—under the aegis of the board's planning and development committee—fashioning and executing a detailed strategy to address the boundary issue, including involvement of a parent advisory committee and a number of public meetings.

POWERFUL RETURN ON YOUR INVESTMENT

These vignettes describe organizations that have put my High-Impact Governing Model™ to work in taking their board's leadership and the board-CEO partnership to the next, higher-impact level. The High-Impact Governing Model™ is based on my twenty-five years of successful experience in working with the boards, CEOs, and executive teams of some 500 nonprofit and public organizations of all shapes and sizes. Experience has taught me that if you seriously apply the High-Impact Governing Model™ your nonprofit or public organization will realize a powerful return on its investment of time and energy in this powerful, thoroughly tested tool:

- **Organizational Security and Growth:** Your organization is secure and thrives in a challenging environment because your "Strategic Governing Team"—the board, CEO, and senior executives—makes high-impact judgments and decisions, successfully addressing the high-stakes strategic and operational issues you're facing, building on your organization's strengths and capitalizing on opportunities for growth and diversification—of programs, revenues, clients, customers, and members.

- **Board Member Ownership and Satisfaction:** Your board members feel strong ownership of—and take great satisfaction in—their governing work, primarily because they have a crystal-clear understanding of their governing role and functions and are involved proactively and creatively in making critical governing decisions and judgments, rather than merely serving as an audience for finished staff work.

• **A Really Solid Board-CEO Working Relationship:** The partnership between your board and CEO is close, productive, and enduring—able to withstand the inevitable stresses and strains of a rapidly changing, challenging world—as a result both of a truly "board-savvy" CEO who takes the lead in helping the board to become a more effective governing body and of the board's meaningful involvement in making critical governing judgments and decisions.

A VIEW FROM THE MOUNTAINTOP

My aim in this book is to provide you with detailed, practical guidance in putting the High-Impact Governing Model™ to work in your nonprofit or public organization. Why? So your board, working closely with your CEO and executive team, can fully realize its tremendous governing potential in practice, generating the three critical benefits I described in the previous section. Before we begin to explore the key elements of the High-Impact Governing Model™, I'd like to share some thoughts about what a nonprofit or public board and CEO actually do when they collaborate in governing. I've spent over a quarter-century thinking about the "business" of governing, drawing on my experience in working with hundreds of boards and CEOs. In my professional opinion, at the highest possible level, governing means answering over and over again four preeminent questions:

1. **The Strategic Question:** Where do we want our organization to head and what do we want it to become over the long run? Who do we envision ourselves serving? What programs and services do we envision ourselves providing? How large

do we envision ourselves becoming? What outcomes do we envision ourselves producing in our environment?

2. The What/Now Question: What do we want our organization to be now and over the coming year, in terms of programs, services, expenditures, revenues, clients, customers, and members?

3. The Accountability Question: How is our organization performing—programmatically, financially, and administratively?

4. The External Relations Question: How do we want to be seen by key stakeholders in our environment, and how can we influence their perceptions? How can we influence stakeholder actions and build closer, more productive ties with potential external partners?

The first question is strategic, and we normally involve the board in some kind of strategic planning process in answering it. The second question is more operational in nature, and we typically involve the board in the operational planning and budget development process in answering it. The third question relates to the board's ultimate accountability for organizational effectiveness and efficiency, and the fourth question relates to maintaining external relationships.

GOVERNING AT A MORE DETAILED LEVEL

Over the past twenty-five years, I've interviewed thousands of nonprofit and public board members, and I always ask my interviewees to describe their governing work. You might be surprised to learn that the response is often shocked silence, after which governing is often vaguely described as "policy making." In reality, making policies—which are essentially broad rules to govern an organization's operations—is only a miniscule part of governing. Of course, your organization needs clear, detailed policies, and a few are so important that they merit your board's attention—for example, determining how large a contract your CEO can sign without board review and approval. But you wouldn't want to be revising policies constantly; that would be the recipe for a collective nervous breakdown.

Keep in mind as you read about the key elements of the High-Impact Governing Model™ that governing basically involves making decisions and judgments about very concrete governing "products" and governing documents. A governing product isn't a final product for your clients, customers, students, or members; it's a product that helps your organization carry out its mission that is important enough to involve your board in producing. For example, when your board adopts an updated values and vision statement or the annual budget, it is making decisions about some of the most important governing products. And when your board reviews a financial report (a document), it is making a judgment about how well your organization is performing financially. That's what governing boils down to: a never-ending stream of decisions and judgments about very concrete products and documents.

FIVE KEY ELEMENTS OF THE MODEL
The remainder of this book focuses on five key elements of the High-Impact Governing Model™:

- **A board-savvy CEO who is a real expert in the field of governance,** who is strongly committed to high-impact board leadership, and who takes the lead in building the board's capacity to do high-impact governing work.

- **A clear, detailed board governing mission describing the board's key governing functions and responsibilities** and meticulously designed processes for involving your board creatively and proactively in such key governing functions as

19

strategic planning, budget development, performance oversight and monitoring, and external relations.

• **A well-designed structure of board standing committees that serve as "governing engines"** in accomplishing the board's detailed governing work.

• **A self-management program aimed at building board member governing knowledge and skills** and strengthening board accountability for its own governing performance.

• **Strong CEO and executive team support** for the board and its standing committees in carrying out their governing functions.

APPENDIX
SUCCESS STORIES

Golden Horizon Homes

Mary Beth Hurley, chair of the board of Golden Horizon Homes, a well-regarded New England institution providing a comprehensive range of services from independent and assisted living to skilled nursing care, stayed around after the board meeting to chat with the four members of the board's governance committee and Mac Mahoney, the executive director. The board had just unanimously adopted the annual operating plan and budget that the board's planning committee had presented. Of course adopting the annual budget wasn't such a big deal in and of itself, but the deep satisfaction that board members almost to a person felt at the conclusion of the budget process was a dramatic departure from past practice.

"When you think about where we were just a year ago," Mary Beth pointed out, "we ought to be breaking out the champagne!" "That's an understatement if I've ever heard one," Mac responded. "I'll never forget how tense you sounded, Mary Beth, when you called me the day after we'd put the budget to bed last year to say that you and the other members of the governance committee needed to meet with me—urgently. And when we got together later that week, I was flabbergasted to learn how frustrated and angry you all were about our budgeting process." "Well, we had a right to be," observed Brendon Behan, one of the longest tenured board members. "Once again, in our typical passive-reactive fashion, we had merely thumbed through a finished tome, asking pretty random, nit-picking questions. Talk about underutilizing a pretty smart and experienced group of board members who really did want to make a difference! We'd had it."

"The great thing is how you responded, Mac," Mary Beth pointed out. "You could easily have gone completely on the defensive and done battle to protect your turf, but, instead, you were willing to sit down with us to figure out how to get us more creatively and proactively involved in the budget process without slipping into micromanagement." "The real turning point was our putting together the board's new planning and program development committee," Brendon chimed in. "Now you had a group of board members to work with in re-designing the budget preparation process, Mac, and the guys and gals on the committee really rose to the occasion." "I agree," said Mac, "I couldn't really have turned the thing around without the active cooperation and support of the committee. You know, the idea of the committee's hosting a half-day board-executive team work session to discuss operational issues that needed to be addressed in preparing the budget wasn't something I recommended to the group. It really did bubble up in our first brainstorming session. And it made a world of difference."

ABC Association

The meeting of the governance committee of the board of the ABC Association, an international trade association in the plastics industry, was coming to an end. "Well, this is a real milestone," board chair Celia Raymond observed as the governance committee—headed by the board chair and including the other standing committee chairs and the CEO—completed its first annual assessment of the board's governing performance. "At the risk of sounding self-congratulatory," she continued, "I think we can be proud that we're actually beginning to play an active role in managing our own performance as a board." "I couldn't agree more," president & CEO Karen Trimble said. "When you made a commitment six months ago to adopt a set of individual board member performance targets and detailed standing committee goals, and to sit down at the end of the year to discuss the board's governing performance, you really did separate yourself out from the pack."

"When you think about it, what we've got here is a real continuous improvement program for the board," Sharon Ransom, chair of the board's monitoring committee, pointed out. "In my committee's area, for example—program and financial performance monitoring—we've done more in today's governance committee meeting than just grading ourselves. We've come up with some really concrete improvements that we can make. I love the idea of experimenting with more creative graphics in my committee's performance reports to the board and testing out quarterly reviews of particular programs." "And I couldn't agree more with all of you that my committee needs to crack the nut of member involvement over the coming year," Mike Bailey, chair of the external/member relations committee observed. "We really delivered in getting a crystal-clear image statement developed, and our survey of member satisfaction generated a ton of useful information for program development, but we just didn't focus in on how to get our members more involved in ABC affairs," he went on.

"OK, it's time to wrap things up," Celia said. "We've got our list of improvement targets for each of our standing committees over the coming year, and we've agreed to devote 30 minutes or so at our quarterly governance committee teleconferences to reviewing progress on the targets. We have a way to go, but no one could accuse us of not taking account-ability for our own governing performance."

Forward Transit

"What's on the community relations committee agenda next month?" asked Agatha Greenwood, general manager of Forward Transit, a four-county transportation agency in the Southeastern U.S., turning to assistant general manager Ray Romanski, whom Agatha had designated as her "chief staff liaison" to the committee. The members of the executive team were ninety minutes into their monthly half-day work session devoted to staffing the Forward Transit board of directors and its standing committees. They'd spent the first 1 ½ hours talk-ing about the agendas of the other two standing committees: planning and development and performance oversight and audit. The bulk of the discussion centered on the design of the annual strategic planning work session that the planning committee would be hosting in February—whether they'd recommend holding a daylong or 1 ½-day session to the com-mittee and if it made sense to recommend that a number of community leaders be invited to participate. The performance oversight and audit agenda was dealt with in under fifteen minutes, since there weren't any significant financial perfor-mance issues to present at the committee meeting, and the external audit process hadn't yet begun.

"Well, Agatha, the biggie we've got to deal with at the next community relations committee meeting," Ray responded, "is getting the Citizens for a Fiscally Sound Forward Transit task force up and running. As we're all keenly aware from the planning and development committee's long-range financial projection at the last board meeting, we've got to get strategies in place as soon as possible to deal with what is beginning to look like a brewing fiscal crisis that's far and away the most serious we've faced since the half-cent sales tax was passed in '01." "Hear, hear Ray, this is the issue of issues right now," Agatha commented, "and there's no way we can do anything really important on the fiscal front—whether, God forbid, it's cutting back service or going for a sales tax increase—without wide and deep public support. Let's face it, we're not a zoo with all those cuddly creatures to warm voters' hearts. Our dear citizens can't possibly feel any affection for one of our buses, and they don't seem to pay any attention to us unless a bus is late or dirty or teens riding home from school entertain their fellow travelers with loud rap music."

The executive team of Forward Transit spent the next hour going over what they'd be recommending at the next community relations committee meeting relative to the task force: the community leaders who'd be invited to serve on the task force; the detailed charge they'd be given; a likely date for the first task force meeting; and the materials that would need to be prepared for that first session. Before adjourning the executive team meeting, Agatha suggested that she and Ray meet with Max Crawford, the committee chair, next week over lunch to go over the agenda. "Normally, I'd just leave it to you, Ray, but this task force is so critical to our future, that it makes sense for me to be involved in reviewing what we'll be recommending with Max to make sure he's on board."

Pleasantville School District

"Believe it or not, my friends, we've done it," an elated Joe Gargary, president of the Pleasantville Board of Education, declared. "We now have new building boundaries. I want to thank my colleagues on the board for their diligence, patience, and good humor throughout this demanding process, and especially the planning and development committee for its outstanding leadership. I also want our superintendent, Liz, and her executive team to know how much we appreciate their excellent support. Finally, I want to recognize the immensely valuable contribution of the parent advisory committee that spent so much time over the past six months mulling over options. If there was ever a team effort, this was it! And now, meeting adjourned. Enjoy the rest of your evening."

Way back in August, when the issue was first seriously discussed at the annual strategic planning work session, no school board member or administrator of the Pleasantville Schools, a rapidly growing suburban district serving 15,000 students, relished having to get involved in re-drawing school boundaries in this small but rapidly growing suburban district in the Midwest. Plenty of parents were sure to be upset—and to share their displeasure with board and executive team members at length—and the prospect of sitting through a series of tense meetings late into the night over the coming months was enough to curdle the blood. But the population shifts going on in the district left them no choice but to bite the proverbial bullet and tackle boundary lines. Just shoving it under the rug would not only be the cowardly course, it would be disastrous.

Fortunately, the participants in the strategic work session agreed that such a complex and potentially explosive strategic issue demanded meticulous planning and management. Accordingly, they took the time to map out the broad outline of a strategy for dealing with the issue and assigned responsibility to the planning and development committee to work with Liz and her team in fleshing out the detailed strategy and to oversee implementation. The fact that boundaries were eventually re-drawn without extraordinary emotional pain and suffering is testimony to the soundness of the strategy that was put in place, including such critical features as: strong oversight by the board's planning and development committee; ample time for review of options at committee meetings; the active involvement of the parent advisory committee from beginning to end; public meetings at key points in the process, at which the facts on population change in the district were shared, boundary options being considered were explained, and input was welcomed.

"You know," president Joe Gargary observed to some colleagues after the board meeting, "I think the leadership of the planning and development committee was THE critical factor in our successfully dealing with boundaries. They didn't just sit back passively and listen to staff reports; they were actively engaged from the get-go, and so by the time of tonight's meeting, they were true owners of the recommendations and real change champions who sold the new boundaries to their colleagues."

2. THE BOARD-SAVVY CEO

THE TEAM CAPTAIN

We expect the chief executive officer, or CEO—the highest ranking, full-time professional staff member reporting directly to the board, going by such titles as "president & CEO," "executive director," "general manager," and "superintendent"—to provide our nonprofit or public organization with capable executive management. We look to our CEO to choose top executives, providing them with direction and assessing their performance, to make sure well-designed administrative systems are in place, etc. But when a nonprofit or public board chooses its CEO, it's also choosing the de facto captain of what I call the Strategic Governing Team: the board, CEO, and senior executives who work directly with the board and its standing committees. Governing really is a collaborative venture, involving intensive, well-orchestrated teamwork to ensure that the decisions and judgments that constitute governing work are made in a full and timely fashion.

Your board, whether it represents the public-at-large, your association's members, or your community, is obviously the most senior member of the Strategic Governing Team—the ultimate authority, judge and decision maker. However, your CEO has to wear the team captain hat in practice, if not theory, if you want the Strategic Governing Team to be healthy, cohesive, and productive. The reason is simple: time (the CEO's and executive team's) and access to resources. No matter how capable, committed, and dedicated board members might be—and experience has taught me they typically are—the fact is that the great majority are part-time, usually unpaid volunteers. They normally have enough trouble coming up with the time to attend board and committee meetings, much less to attend public functions, speak in appropriate forums, and sometimes even raise money. Only the CEO has the time (including senior staff's) to plan for, manage, and support the Strategic Governing Team.

YOU NEED A BOARD-SAVVY TEAM CAPTAIN

Behind every really high-impact governing board that I've worked with or observed over the past twenty-five years has always been a truly "board-savvy" CEO who serves as an effective captain of the Strategic Governing Team. Every board needs one, and so one of your board's most important responsibilities is to choose a CEO who really is "board-savvy." However, sad to say, many boards in my experience extensively interview CEO candidates without asking probing questions aimed at determining CEO candidates' board-savvyness. It isn't hard to come up with pertinent questions. For example, a school board I worked with a couple of years ago that was engaged in interviewing superintendent candidates came up with such questions as:

- "Would you please define in detail what you think 'governing' means?"

- "Broadly speaking, how do you see the board's role as different from the superintendent's?"

- "What concrete steps did you take to help your last school board develop its governing capacity?"

- "What are the key characteristics of a really solid board-superintendent partnership?"

- "How do you see yourself working with our board chair?"

Unfortunately, in my experience many boards just don't recognize the need to make sure their CEO is board-savvy. If they luck out, they end up with a CEO who's board-savvy; but if they don't, the cost can be quite high, in terms not only of lower-impact governing, but also an unstable board-CEO working relationship. The profile of the board-savviest CEOs I've worked with over the years includes the following four attributes; they:

1. Bring the right attitude to the governing business: welcoming and celebrating strong board leadership and a close, positive, and productive board-CEO partnership.

2. Make governing a top-tier priority: mastering—and devoting a healthy dollop of time to—the governing function.

3. Wear the Chief Board Developer hat—taking accountability for helping the board build its governing capacity.

4. Pay close attention to the psychological and emotional facet of their working relationship with their board, coming up with practical ways to provide their board members with ego satisfaction and to turn them into passionate owners of their governing work.

Let's take a brief look at each of these attributes.

THE RIGHT ATTITUDE

I've learned to spot board-savvy and un-savvy CEOs pretty soon after meeting them, just by listening to them talk about their boards and the governing process generally. Let's see if you can tell the difference:

CEO A: You know, I stay out of the board's business—policy making—and I expect them to stay out of mine—executive management and administration. I'm always keenly aware of the danger that they'll begin to get bogged down in details and become micromanagers rather than the governors they're supposed to be, so I make sure that I bring them finished staff recommendations and try to keep them from digging too deeply in the details. You might call me a kind of border patrol officer, always on the alert to keep them from crossing over into my territory. They're a bright and well-meaning group overall, and I don't think they mean to do any harm, but I've got to watch them like a hawk or their tentacles will be wrapped around things that rightly belong in my CEO bailiwick.

CEO B: I see myself in two ways vis-à-vis my board. First, my board is obviously a precious asset, consisting of the experience, knowledge, expertise, perspectives, and connections that board members bring to the board room. One of my most important CEO jobs is to make sure that this precious asset is fully deployed on behalf of my organization: that my board really does make a difference in organizational affairs. Second, I see myself as a partner with my board, sharing the work of governing. Of course, there has to be some division of labor in governing areas such as planning, but, frankly, you can't draw a line with something called "policy making" on one side and management on the other. I've got to be an active participant in the work of governing, and a close partner with my board, and this means not only helping them make effective judgments and decisions, but also making sure that they really own their governing work and find it satisfying.

I assume you chose CEO B as the board-savvier of the two. CEO B obviously sees his or her board as a resource to be fully tapped in leading the organization, not just as a damage control challenge. This board-savvy CEO knows that governing is a CEO function, not just the board's, and that partnership is the name of the governing game. And CEO B recognizes that he or she has to take accountability for the quality of the board's governing experience, aggressively helping the board accomplish its governing work.

If you are a CEO or CEO-aspirant and you put your money on CEO A, you face a stark choice: either seek attitude readjustment assistance or look forward to a pretty rocky, and probably short, relationship with your board!

TOP PRIORITY

The board-savvy CEO believes that governing is a top CEO priority and that governing is a true CEO function (albeit shared with the board). Concretely, this means spending lots of time on governing matters, becoming a real expert in the governing "business," and systematically managing the "governing program." The board-savviest CEOs I've seen and worked with over the years tend to put somewhere between twenty and twenty-five percent of their time into working with their board, and I'm talking quality time, not just schmoozing: fashioning strategies for strengthening the board's governing capacity; developing agendas for committee and board meetings; chairing regular meetings of the executive team dedicated to board agenda development; ensuring that materials going to the board are high-quality; formally and informally communicating with board members on a regular basis; and the like.

KNOWING GOVERNING INSIDE-OUT

In addition to making a significant commitment of time to governing matters, board-savvy CEOs take the trouble to become experts in the rapidly developing field of public and nonprofit governance, regularly reading periodicals and books focusing on board leadership and the board-CEO partnership and attending educational sessions at conferences. Indeed, they think of governing as one of the core CEO competencies, along with such critical functions as strategic planning, financial management, and external relations. Because they systematically educate themselves in this complex and dynamic field, board-savvy CEOs learn to distrust what I call "fallacious little nuggets of wisdom" that, although they are often touted as scientific truth, turn out on closer examination to be wrong-headed and often quite damaging.

A rather minor example would be the counsel that boards should always be sent "finished staff work." Really board-savvy CEOs well know that, while some work should be finished before reaching the boardroom, if a more important governing "product" such as the annual budget goes to the board in finished form, the potential for serious board ownership of the product is virtually nil. After all, this late in the budget preparation process, not long before the balanced budget must be adopted, what recourse does the board have but to thumb through the document making minor adjustments and asking relatively trivial questions? To open the budget document up to serious questioning at this point in the game would be risking chaos.

To take a much more egregious example, if I've heard once I've heard a hundred times that small boards are more effective governing bodies than bigger ones. Although "big" and "small" are relative terms, the small-board advocates often recommend that a board not be larger than nine members, and they react with horror to the thought of twenty-five or more potential micromanagers gathering in the boardroom. True, smaller boards are attractive from a narrow efficiency perspective—requiring less care and feeding and being more likely to secure a quorum at meetings—and they are easier to turn into cohesive governing bodies. But really board-savvy CEOs know that board downsizing can come at a high cost that should be seriously considered before jumping aboard the small-board bandwagon.

For example, the larger a board, the more diversity you can build into your governing process—socially, culturally, and in terms of knowledge, experience, and connections with the wider world. Larger boards have more room to add key stakeholder representatives (a stakeholder is an organization with which it makes sense to maintain a working relationship because of the stakes involved) as a tried and true way to build alliances and to enhance your board's political clout.

THE GOVERNING PROGRAM

A really board-savvy CEO I worked with years ago—head of a large nonprofit retirement community—shared a trick of the trade with me that I've subsequently recommended to many other CEOs: treating governing as a formal program that the CEO consciously and systematically manages as the program "director"—behind the scenes, of course, since many board members are likely not to embrace being treated as a kind of program. This CEO set clear goals for strengthening her board's governing capacity, fashioned strategies to accomplish these goals, and rigorously monitored progress in carrying out the strategies.

For example, she set as one of her targets helping the board develop a stronger role in the agency's operational planning and budget development process, working closely with the board's planning committee. Her strategy included such steps as convincing the committee chair to hold a special "pre-budget" work session at the beginning of the budget cycle, at which department heads identified and described operational issues meriting attention in fashioning next year's budget, and the planning committee's holding two follow-up board work sessions to review preliminary budget figures before casting the document in bronze.

CHIEF BOARD DEVELOPER

When we talk about "board development" we mean developing your board's effectiveness as a governing organization, primarily by: clarifying your board's governing role, fine-tuning your board's governing structure, and mapping out processes for involving your board in such critical governing functions as strategic planning and performance monitoring. Board development is a never-ending process since boards, like any other organization, can always improve—in fact, should always be improving, taking advantage of advances in the field of non-profit and public governance. Ironically, many board members, in my experience, resist—or at least don't enthusiastically welcome—being developed. My take on this is that they, like other normal human beings, fear change—even if unconsciously—primarily because of the possibility of extreme discomfort, or, worse, failure and the accompanying ego deflation. As a result, board development tends to be more of a human, than a technical, challenge.

You want to keep in mind that board development can take place in a number of ways. If you have a well-designed board standing committee structure (see Chapter 4), your committees can serve as continuous development vehicles in their respective functional areas. For example, your board's planning committee can work closely with your CEO in designing a strategic planning process that builds in a stronger front-end guidance role for the board, perhaps through participation in a strategic planning work session kicking off the planning process. And your performance monitoring committee can work with your CEO in developing more effective programmatic performance reports to the board.

In the absence of a well-designed committee structure, many boards and their CEOs have used a day-long governance retreat as a vehicle for identifying needed improvements in their board's governing role, structure and processes. Others have employed a governance task force to come up with practical recommendations for strengthening their board's governing capacity. Whatever the approach taken to building your board's governing capacity, board-savvy CEOs know that it's unrealistic to expect their board members to play the leading role in board development for the simple reason that they don't have the time to devote. When serious board development occurs, it's almost always driven by a board-savvy CEO wearing the Chief Board Developer hat who:

1. Takes the lead in getting board members interested in—and committed to—developing the board's governing capacity by, for example, sharing pertinent articles on governance with board members, and by encouraging board members to attend educational sessions on governance at national and state conferences.

2. Convinces the board to participate in a particular board development process, such as a governance retreat or task force.

3. Is knowledgeable enough about the field of nonprofit and public governance to help the board make sensible, well-informed decisions about such important questions as the standing committees that should be established to help the board accomplish its governing work.

4. Ensures that the board development process is successful by providing strong support, both during the process and in implementing the recommendations coming out of it. For example, if your board's governance task force recommends that the board adopt governing performance targets and regularly monitor its own performance, the board-savvy CEO will ensure that the targets actually get set and that the monitoring process is established.

KEEPING THE FRAGILE BOND FROM FRAYING

Several years ago, I was working with the council and city manager of a middle-sized suburban community. One day, I walked into the city manager's office and found him holding his head in his hands, looking distraught. "For heaven's sake, what's happened?" I asked. "Look at this," he said, pushing a piece of paper across his desk, "I've just received my annual evaluation, and I'm in shock." As I worked my way down the form, I was puzzled by his reaction, since on one criterion after another—financial planning, budgeting, inventory management, you name it—he was rated "superior" or "excellent."

But when I reached the comments section at the bottom, I understood why he was ashen-faced. What it said in so many words was, "You're great at the technical aspects of the job, but we can't continue working with you—it's too painful. You always have to be right, and you treat us like we're an audience for your impeccably-done staff work, rather than an influential leadership body." Within a couple of months, this technically accomplished but obviously board-unsavvy CEO was gone. The lesson I learned was valuable: No matter how smart and technically capable a CEO is, neglecting the "soft"—or human —side of the board-CEO partnership isn't a recipe for success.

The board-savviest CEOs I've worked with over the years know, first, that their working partnership with their board is always fragile—prone to erode quickly if not systematically maintained and nurtured, and, second, that maintaining this fragile bond requires paying really close attention to the psychological and emotional dimension of the relationship. Keeping the partnership healthy is no mean feat, when you think of the individuals and the circumstances at the top of your organization. To start with, board members tend to be ambitious, high-achieving, hard-driving individuals who can be impatient and at times imperious. They come to the boardroom with high expectations, and they don't suffer disappointment gladly. When you add to the mix a rapidly changing, always challenging world that hurls one issue after another at boards and their CEOs, you can easily understand why the board-CEO bond tends to fray.

TWO SIMPLE STRATEGIES

I've seen really board-savvy CEOs employ two simple but effective strategies to keep their partnership with the board healthy:

1. They take advantage of opportunities to provide their board members with ego satisfaction. For example, one CEO I know routinely turns speaking invitations over to board members, rather than just accepting them herself. Another goes out of his way to involve board members in meetings with key external stakeholders, including the media. A superintendent I was working with, for example, made a point of inviting her school board president to several meetings with the county executive on regional economic development issues. And, of course, making sure board members are regularly publicly recognized for their efforts—say, in the monthly newsletter—is a low cost-high yield tactic.

2. And these board-savvy CEOs are always on the lookout for ways to foster feelings of ownership among their board members. One of the most effective ownership-building strategies, which I discuss in detail in the next chapter, is to design into the strategic and operational planning processes opportunities for early board input and guidance. This is the polar opposite of the old-fashioned approach of just presenting the board with a finished plan at the tail-end of the process, turning board members into a passive audience while building absolutely no ownership.

3. THE BOARD'S MISSION AND GOVERNING WORK

WHAT'S THE BOARD'S REASON FOR BEING?

Effective organizations are guided by a clear mission that tells one and all why they're in business—what they fundamentally do and who they do it for—and within the framework of this mission, they map out operational processes aimed at translating that mission into practice. A board is by definition an organization within the wider organization it's responsible for governing: a formally established, permanent group of people working together to achieve a common purpose—to govern. So it stands to reason that boards, like all other organizations, need a crystal clear mission. Otherwise, how can they know that their members are engaged in doing the right governing work? In other words, if your board doesn't have a firm grasp of the WHAT—its intended governing outcomes—then there's no sensible way of dealing with the HOW—mapping out the processes that board members need to be involved in to translate this or that element of the mission into practice.

You've probably heard it said that the ideal mission is a one or two-sentence statement—a pithy paragraph—that captures your organization's reason for being in a neat nutshell. That's fine if your intent is to inspire staff and pique the public's imagination, but a board needs a more detailed functional statement to guide and drive the development of its governing processes. Recognizing this, an increasing number of public and nonprofit boards around the country have in recent years adopted a detailed "Governing Mission" to guide their governing labors. Let's look at a real life example.

MAPPING OUT A GOVERNING MISSION

A few months ago at a special work session, the board of directors, CEO, and senior managers of a large, well-respected nonprofit agency in upstate New York that provides services to children with mental disabilities adopted by resolution a "Board Governing Mission" spelling out the major governing responsibilities of the board. The resolution made clear how seriously the agency's Strategic Governing Team took the Governing Mission, solemnizing their commitment to playing a high-impact governing role:

> Whereas, the Board of Directors...is firmly committed to functioning as a high-impact governing body, providing the...Home with the strong leadership required to ensure its future effectiveness in a changing, challenging world.

> Whereas, providing such high-impact leadership requires a clearly defined Board of Directors Governing Role.

> Be it resolved that: The...Home Board of Directors adopts the Board Governing Mission...and directs that this Governing Mission be periodically updated and that it serve as a framework for further developing the Board's governing work, structure, and processes over time in the interest of high-impact governing.

The Governing Mission that was attached to the resolution had been brainstormed in a governance retreat several months earlier and subsequently augmented and polished by the Governance Task Force that ultimately recommended its adoption. The Governing Mission consists of five elements completing the sentence that begins, The Board of Directors:

> 1. Serves as the steward and guardian of the...Home's values, vision, mission, and resources.

2. Plays a leading, proactive role in the...Home's strategic decision making, and in setting strong, clear strategic directions and priorities for all...operating units and programs.

3. Monitors the...Home's operational performance (both programmatic and financial) against clearly defined performance targets.

4. Ensures that the...Home's image and relationships with the wider community and key stakeholders are positive and that they contribute to the...Home's success in carrying out its mission.

5. Makes sure that the...Home possesses the financial and other resources necessary to realize its vision and carry out its mission fully.

SERVING AS A PRACTICAL TOOL

This nonprofit children's services agency and many other nonprofit and public organizations around the country have been able to put such high-level board job descriptions to good use, primarily because their Governing Missions consist of specific points, rather than being just a perfunctory pithy paragraph of two or three sentences. For example, they have used their Governing Missions:

> • **As a credibility builder**: demonstrating to key stakeholders in the wider world, including foundations and other funders, and—in the case of associations, to their members—that they know what governing is all about and take it very seriously. "We're well governed, and you can rest assured that giving us money and other kinds of support will be a safe investment" is the message being sent, and that's critically important in today's world, when the public-at-large, funding organizations, and increasingly Congress and state legislatures are paying close attention to the accountability of nonprofit and public organizations.

• **As an orientation tool**: making sure that incoming board members understand the board's key responsibilities before they jump into the governing process.

• **As a recruiting magnet** to attract interest in serving on the board: clearly communicating to potential board members that serving on our board won't be the same-old, same-old experience; rather, we stand above the pack in knowing exactly what we're doing, and our board is well worth the investment of your precious volunteer time and energy. Not only will your work on our board be meaningful, but you'll also acquire valuable governing knowledge and skills that you can apply to other boards you serve on.

• **As a guide** to mapping out the board's detailed governing processes and **a measuring stick** to assess the board's governing performance.

USING THE MEASURING STICK

The last point deserves some elaboration. Take one of the elements of the Governing Mission of the children's services agency cited above: "Ensures that the...Home's image and relationships with the wider community and key stakeholders are positive and that they contribute to the...Home's success in carrying out its mission." In the first place, it's clear that this board must play a role in external relations since that's an element of its Governing Mission. The Mission doesn't say exactly what role, but there's no question the role must be developed by mapping out processes for board involvement in external relations, for example, by having board members speak in external forums on behalf of the agency. Having this element in the Governing Mission also suggests that the board should consider establishing a standing committee on external relations to carry the ball in this governing area.

And the Governing Mission element "plays a leading, proactive role in the. . .Home's strategic decision making, and in setting strong, clear strategic directions and priorities for all...operating units and programs" mandates the Home's board of directors be involved in some kind of formal strategic planning process. The Mission doesn't specify the process, but there's no question that a strategic planning process needs to be developed. There's also a strong argument for the board to employ a planning committee to take the lead in this critical functional area.

THE KEYS TO HIGHER-IMPACT GOVERNING

You'll recall that the work of governing essentially involves your board's making judgments and decisions about very concrete governing "products" and documents—values and vision statements, budgets, financial reports, and the like. These judgments and decisions flow along broad governing streams: the board's management of its own governing operations; strategic and operational planning; performance oversight; and external relations. The two most powerful keys to developing your board's governing capacity, within the framework of your board's detailed Governing Mission, are:

1. Well-defined processes for board involvement in making these judgments and decisions; and

2. A well-designed board standing committee structure that matches the streams of governing judgments and decisions.

Over the years when I've come across public and nonprofit boards that are falling well short of their governing potential—and I've seen some pretty dysfunctional governing bodies in my time—I've heard frustrated board members and CEOs say that if they could just get the "right" people on the board, governing performance would dramatically improve. In my experience, the people on the board are almost never the problem.

In fact, I've never in all my years in the business come across a nonprofit or public board that absolutely had to add new members in order to take its governing to the next, higher-impact level. To be sure, beefing up your board's composition—enriching the mix of experience, expertise, and connections that board members bring to the boardroom—can turn your board into a more influential governing body and help it make better governing judgments and decisions, but well-designed process and structure are *the preeminent keys* to high-impact governing. I take a close look at process in this chapter and structure in the next.

DESIGNING BOARD GOVERNING PROCESSES

Here are four "little golden rules" to follow in mapping out your board's involvement in the detailed work of governing, within the framework of your Governing Mission:

1. Use your board's standing committees as what you might call "design vehicles"—forums where the board members on a particular committee can work in a relatively relaxed setting with your CEO and executive team members in mapping out what the committee and full board should do when in, for example, the strategic planning process or in monitoring organizational performance.

2. In designing processes for committee and full board involvement in particular governing streams, make sure that you take advantage of advances in the field of nonprofit and public governance and related fields, rather than reinventing the proverbial wheel or just going with strong-spoken and assertive board members' pet approaches. For example, in recent years we've seen dramatic advances in the very important field of strategic planning that your board's planning committee and the CEO will want to pay close attention to in working out the board's role in making strategic decisions.

3. On the technical front, you've got to make sure that any process for board involvement that your organization employs actually produces the intended outcomes in a full and timely fashion. For example, you will want your annual operational planning and budgeting process to produce an operating plan containing detailed, measurable performance targets and a balanced revenue and expenditure budget that your board can adopt before the new fiscal year begins. If you can't get a balanced budget adopted on time, you're in deep trouble.

4. But making sure your design for board involvement in a particular governing area like planning is technically sound isn't enough by a long shot. If you want your board members to emerge from a process feeling strongly committed to the outcomes that it's generated (for example, a detailed operating plan and budget), you've got to make sure that the involvement of your board members turns them into *owners*. There are two tried and true ways to build feelings of ownership among board members. First, you can make sure that they play a meaningful role, which basically means that their input is serious and makes a real difference in shaping the outcomes a particular process is intended to produce. Second, you can ensure that board member involvement is proactive, which means that it is early enough to shape and guide the ultimate outcomes. As you surely have learned by this time in your leadership career, a key feature of any board that operates in the passive/reactive mode—merely thumbing through a finished product, whether it's a vision statement or a budget—is a complete lack of ownership, and the consequent absence of strong commitment.

A CASE EXAMPLE: STRATEGIC PLANNING DESIGN

Not too long ago, a really board-savvy CEO and I worked closely with the board's planning and program development committee in designing a detailed strategic planning process for this national healthcare association. Being really board-savvy, this CEO took the trouble to familiarize herself with recent dramatic developments in the wild and wonderful world of strategic planning before she jumped into designing a planning process with the committee. She wanted to make sure that whatever they came up with was truly contemporary and that board members didn't waste precious time, energy, and money participating in yesterday's outmoded process in dealing with today's and tomorrow's challenges.

As you probably know, strategic planning has moved well beyond the kind of old-time, long-range comprehensive planning for arbitrary and meaningless periods such as three and five years (remember Soviet five-year agricultural and industrial plans?) that used to be so popular. This board-savvy CEO learned that the for-profit and nonprofit organizations that tend to thrive in today's rapidly changing, always challenging environment don't produce monster "tractor plans" by compiling detailed program plans that project the present into the future. Rather, they focus on identifying strategic issues (change challenges in the form of high-stakes opportunities and threats) and fashioning "change initiatives" to address the highest-priority issues — completely separate from running their ongoing programs and operations.

Donning her "chief human relations officer hat," this board-savvy CEO also knew that she and the planning and program development committee needed to design a strategic planning process that was more than just technically up-to-date; board members needed and deserved to be involved in ways that ensured their strong commitment to the strategic decisions and plans that the process was intended to produce. The following important features of the process they came up with, which has subsequently been successfully applied, illustrate the close attention they paid to both technical and human factors:

• Daylong Strategic Work Session
The annual planning cycle is kicked off every year by a daylong "strategic work session," which the planning and program development committee hosts. The session is opened with two formal presentations, using PowerPoint: conditions and trends that are pertinent to the association's vision and mission (which members of the planning and program development committee present) and operational performance over the past year (which members of the board's performance monitoring committee present). Breakout groups led by board members are employed as a device to generate pertinent information and questions and to ensure active board member participation, providing an opportunity for open-ended input and building feelings of ownership early in the process. For example, among the breakout groups they used at last year's strategic work session were "Values/Vision Update," "Organizational Strengths and Weaknesses Assessment," "Opportunities for Growth and Diversification," "Identification and Analysis of Important Stakeholder Relationships," and "Emerging New Member Needs."

• Careful Follow-Through
Systematic follow-up that the planning and program development committee spearheads has been built into the process, including:

• The committee's analysis of the strategic issues that were identified in the strategic work session (drawing on the detailed analysis done by the CEO and her executive team), the identification of the highest priority issues, and the recommendation of the issues to the board.

• The committee's determination of the vehicles to be employed in fashioning "strategic change initiatives" to address the selected issues, on the recommendation of the CEO and her executive team, for example: a task force comprised exclusively of staff; a task force consisting of representatives of the association's members; a consultant retained to develop an initiative.

• The committee's overseeing the process of developing strategic change initiatives and conducting interim and final reviews of the initiatives.

• **Review of Preliminary Drafts**
The full Board has opportunities to review preliminary versions of the strategic change initiatives in special work sessions that are conducted by the planning and program development committee, and input from such work sessions is conveyed to the bodies developing the initiatives so that board input is reflected in the final versions.

This carefully designed, highly participatory process is the polar opposite of the old-time approach of presenting a finished strategic plan to a board, which at the tail end of the process is relegated to merely thumbing through a document that board members have played a minor role, if any, in shaping—a recipe for slight ownership and little if any commitment.

4. BOARD STANDING COMMITTEES

THE APRIL COMMITTEE MEETING

"**O**K, we've reached agreement on the steps we're going to follow in selecting a new external audit firm, which you're going to write up for our final review and adoption at the June committee meeting, right?" said Abigail Stevens, chair of the performance monitoring and audit committee, turning to the "chief staff liaison" who staffed the committee, Hank Carlson, vice president of finance and CFO of the Sunny Acres Retirement Community. Abigail and the other five board members making up the committee, along with CEO June Goodwin, Hank and a couple of other executive team members attending the April meeting, had just gone through a really probing, 30-minute discussion of the criteria that they should focus on in hiring a new external audit firm, and they had about an hour left on the rest of the agenda: review of the bi-monthly programmatic and financial performance reports that would be presented at the next board meeting and discussion of a revised contracting policy that June and her team were recommending.

"Take us through the performance reports, Hank and Sally," Abigail said, turning to the CFO and the vice president for program operations, Sally Goldwin. Before they began going through the reports, Abigail pointed out that they should leave a full half-hour for discussion of the recommended contracting policy update, since it included a provision raising the ceiling on contracts June could sign without board approval (so long as it was budgeted) from $5,000 to $20,000. "I think we're likely to spend more than one meeting looking at the contracting policy," Abigail observed, "since this is potentially the most controversial recommendation we've taken to the board since the committee was created a year ago, and I want to make sure we've got a strong case."

Getting the performance monitoring and audit committee, along with the other three committees making up the board's new structure—board operations, planning and development, and community relations—up and running had been a daunting challenge, in light of board members' extremely busy lives and day-to-day demands on CEO June Goodwin and her team. Another challenge had been some long-time board members' attachment to the former structure of old-fashioned, narrowly focused "silo" committees corresponding not to governing functions, but to particular program areas and administrative functions, such as "personnel," "assisted living," "skilled nursing," and "buildings and grounds." But all four committees were functioning well, just as the governance task force that had recommended their creation a year ago had promised, and board members could already see an impressive payoff.

Board members felt a growing sense of empowerment, and there's no question board meetings had become more interesting and productive. What a difference it made, for example, to have members of the performance monitoring and audit committee present the programmatic and financial performance reports at board meetings, employing attractive, easy-to-understand graphics. The PowerPoint bar charts comparing actual to budgeted expenditures were a particular hit—a big step forward from the confusing rows and columns of numbers that the board had been getting for years. Having committee members do the reporting ensured deeper understanding of Sunny Acres' financial position, and it was also quite ego-satisfying—certainly more than just sitting and listening to the CFO go over the financials.

POTENTIALLY POWERFUL GOVERNING ENGINES

If you'd asked me about the importance of board standing committees twenty years ago, I wouldn't have advised you to pay much attention to them. Committees certainly didn't make my top-ten list of factors that influence governing board effectiveness, and there's certainly nothing theoretically interesting about a committee structure. Experience has educated me, as it always should, and now I number well-designed committees among the top five determinants of governing board success, producing powerful benefits for nonprofit and public boards:

• Committees enable a board to divide the very complex work of governing into "chewable" chunks, making it possible for board members to acquire in-depth knowledge and expertise in the broad governing functions, such as planning and performance monitoring, as well as providing board members with a greater opportunity for proactive involvement in shaping important governing judgments and decisions than is possible in board plenary sessions.

• As a consequence of their enhanced governing knowledge and expertise, along with their more proactive involvement, board members feel much stronger ownership of, and commitment to, their governing work.

• Well-designed committees ensure thorough preparation for full board meetings, thereby elevating the level of full board discussion and decision making.

• In addition to preparing for full board meetings, standing committees can serve as a vehicle for continuously fine-tuning and improving the detailed governing work in their respective governing areas, such as board self-management and performance monitoring.

COMMITTEES MUST BE WELL-DESIGNED

In the organizational development business, there's a classic rule that has proved its usefulness in practice: Organizational form must correspond to organizational function if you want that organization to succeed at carrying out its mission over the long run. Where boards are concerned, this means that the board's standing committees must correspond to the broad governing functions (the streams of decisions and judgments that the board makes) of the board. As you know, there are basically four board governing streams: the board's direction and management of its own operations as a governing body; strategic and operational planning; financial and programmatic performance monitoring; and external relations. Following the form follows function rule, you will obviously want to organize your board's standing committees by these streams.

Another committee design principle that has proved to be very beneficial in practice is to make sure that your board's standing committee structure possesses what I call "horizontal discipline," which means that each standing committee's purview is organization-wide, cutting across all programs and administrative functions. Strategic and operational planning is for the whole organization, not specific parts of it. Performance monitoring is done for all programs and administrative units, and so on.

I'm not certain why many boards ended up with the old-time silo structure of narrowly focused programmatic and administrative committees, such as the conference or education committee of an association; the curriculum and instruction or personnel committee of a school district; the rail operations or paratransit committee of a public transportation agency; the skilled nursing or assisted living committee of an aging services nonprofit. But I do know that the old-time silo structure is a real enemy of high-impact governing, because it:

> • Narrowly focuses the attention of board members, making organization-wide analysis and comparative decision-making well-nigh impossible and creating a clear and present danger that the good of the whole organization will be sacrificed to parochial concerns.

• Uses board members as in-depth technical advisers in specific areas, rather than as true governors of the whole organization.

• And quite often actually turns board members into passionate advocates for particular programs (for example, I've witnessed silo committee chairs vie with each other for a larger slice of the budget pie for their particular programs, irrespective of the good of the overall organization).

A MODEL STRUCTURE

A large, highly respected, and growing local nonprofit providing services to the blind and visually impaired has put in place a structure of five standing committees that match the broad governing functions of the board and promote cross-cutting horizontal discipline (see Figure A, Committee Organization Chart):

• **The Board Operations Committee**
Headed by the Board Chair and consisting of the Board Chair-Elect, Treasurer, Secretary, and Immediate Past Chair, the Chairs of the Planning and Program Development, Performance Oversight and Monitoring, and External Relations/Resource Development Committees, and the President & CEO as an ex officio member, the Board Operations Committee is essentially a committee on the management and coordination of the Board of Directors. In this capacity, the Board Operations Committee is responsible for continuous development of the board's governing capacity, board human resource development (nominating candidates to fill board vacancies and developing board member governing skills), the coordination of board and standing committee operations, and for maintenance of the Board-President & CEO working relationship, including annual evaluation of CEO perfor-

mance and determination of CEO compensation. The Board Operations Committee may take action on behalf of the full board in true emergency situations when it is not feasible to assemble a quorum of the full Board.

• **Planning and Program Development Committee**
The Planning and Program Development Committee is responsible for working closely with the President & CEO in designing and overseeing a strategic planning process that will enable the organization to deal effectively with strategic issues facing the corporation in today's rapidly changing world. The Planning and Program Development Committee is also responsible for coordinating the board's participation in the organization's operational planning and budget preparation process and for recommending adoption of the annual budget to the board.

• **Performance Oversight and Monitoring Committee**
The board's Performance Oversight and Monitoring Committee is responsible for working closely with the president & CEO in designing programmatic and financial performance reports that are appropriate for board review and for monitoring the performance of all of the organization's programs and administrative units. This committee is also responsible for reviewing and recommending revised and new operational policies meriting the board's attention (such as contracting and procurement policies).

• **External Relations/Resource Development Committee**
The board's External Relations/Resource Development Committee is concerned both with public relations and fund raising, including donor relations. It is responsible for clarifying the organization's desired public image in the eyes of clients, the public-at-large and key stakeholders; for overseeing the formulation of strategies to promote the image; for maintaining effective communication and work-

ing relationships with important stakeholders, including actual and prospective donors; for recommending policy positions in the governmental relations/legislative arena; and for overseeing the formulation of strategies to promote active volunteer involvement in Lighthouse affairs. The External Relations/Resource Development Committee is also responsible for ensuring that the organization possesses the financial resources required to carry out its strategic and operational plans in a full and timely fashion. In this regard, at the top of the committee's list of priorities is implementation of the organization's fund-raising and endowment building strategy.

• The Audit Committee

Reporting directly to the Board of Directors, the Audit Committee consists of three members who are nominated by the Board Operations Committee and elected by the board, and who are not members of the Board Operations Committee. The Audit Committee is responsible for selecting the organization's external audit firm and for overseeing the external audit process. In this capacity, the Audit Committee reviews the annual audit report, recommends board action as necessary in response to the audit report, and monitors implementation of recommended actions. The Audit Committee meets with the external auditors at least once annually, conducting a portion of that meeting in private session with neither the CEO nor any other staff present. In nominating members to serve on the Audit Committee, the Board Operations Committee ensures that nominees possess the training and experience required to carry out their oversight responsibilities.

Figure A
STANDING COMMITTEE
ORGANIZATION CHART

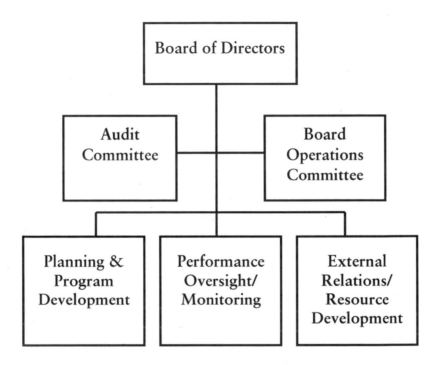

INSTITUTIONALIZING COMMITTEES

Your organization can take three major steps to ensure that your new board's standing committees are firmly established: (1) have your board adopt the committee structure by resolution; (2) have your board also adopt by resolution a set of detailed guidelines to govern operation of the standing committees; and (3) put in place an executive staff committee support structure and process (discussed in detail in Chapter 6). I recommend that the section of your organization's bylaws that deals with standing committees consist of only two sections: (1) providing that the board can establish by resolution any standing committees it needs to carry out its governing responsibilities; and (2) describing the composition and functions of the committee responsible for the board's operations (whether called board operations, governance or executive).

Among the most important guidelines adopted by the board of the agency serving the blind and visually impaired whose structure is described above are:

- The Board Chair will appoint the chairs and members of the Planning and Program Development, Performance Oversight and Monitoring, and External Relations Committees.

- Each Board member should be assigned to one (but only one) of the standing committees. (Note an exception: that standing committee chairs—other than the chair of the Audit Committee—also serve on the Board Operations Committee.)

- Only members of the Board of Directors may serve on the Board's standing committees. However, non-board volunteers can serve on any ad hoc subcommittees and task forces that the standing committees establish and oversee.

- All matters coming to the full board should go through the appropriate standing committee and be introduced by committee members. No action items should be introduced directly to the full board, without having come through the appropriate board standing committee, and all reports to the board should be made by standing committee members (with the sole exceptions of the regular President & CEO report to the board and when non-board advisory committee members or staff members present special briefings under the aegis of the standing committees).

AN OBSTACLE TO WATCH OUT FOR

As you plan to put a new board standing committee structure in place you should be aware that you might have to contend with some pretty emotional opposition from one or more longer-tenured board members who have become emotionally wedded to existing silo committees. The reason is simple: they've learned to exert influence through the traditional structure, which they feel comfortable with and which provides them with considerable ego satisfaction. Replacing traditional committees with a more contemporary structure, therefore, will appear to threaten the hard-earned influence of these senior board members. A tried and true strategy for dealing with such opposition is to designate the more influential potential opponents as chairs of the new committees, thereby turning them into owners of change. If that isn't feasible, then at the very least take the trouble to make sure that they are given the committee assignments they want.

5. BOARD SELF-MANAGEMENT

SHARED ACCOUNTABILITY

Y ou'll recall from the discussion in Chapter 2 that a key feature of my High-Impact Governing Model™ is shared accountability for the governing function— among the members of what I call the Strategic Governing Team: the board; the chief executive officer; and executive staff members who work with the board and its committees. Another important feature of the Model is the CEO's leadership role as the de facto "captain" of the Strategic Governing Team, in this role serving as the Chief Board Capacity Builder and ensuring that the board and its standing committees are provided with strong staff support.

However, even though governing is a team effort that depends on strong CEO leadership and support, one of the important characteristics of really high-impact nonprofit and public boards is their taking explicit accountability for managing themselves as governing bodies. Experience has taught me that four keys are critical to effective board self-management:

1. A responsible board standing committee

2. Meticulous management and coordination of board operations

3. A fully developed board human resource development function

4. And a fully developed board performance management function

RESPONSIBLE COMMITTEE

I learned early in my career as a consultant and teacher in the field of nonprofit and public governance that if an important governing function isn't assigned to a particular board standing committee, the likelihood of its being well-handled ranges from slight to nil. I've served on more than one board, and you probably have too, that never could get around to monitoring the governing performance of its members, even though every so often one board member or another would point out the need. Why? Well, the kind of high-achieving, ambitious, talented people who tend to populate nonprofit and public boards are typically avid fans of, and advocates for, setting targets and measuring their achievement. That's one of the reasons they've succeeded in their business or profession and have been tapped to serve on the board. So attitude hasn't been the problem. The real culprit, in my experience, is almost always the absence of a committee responsible for developing and implementing the function.

One committee is ideally positioned to play a hands-on role in board self-management: what is usually called "board operations" or "governance" these days and was traditionally known as the "executive" committee. Headed by the board chair and consisting of the other standing committee chairs and the CEO, and sometimes one or more other board officers, such as the vice-chair and the secretary-treasurer, the governance or board operations committee brings together the people who are ideally qualified to handle the board-self management function.

METICULOUS MANAGEMENT AND COORDINATION
The following account, which is based on many meetings that I've sat in on over the years, illustrates how your board operations or governance committee can play an active role in managing and coordinating your board's operations:

Case Study: A Governance Committee in Action
"Since we're all here, let's get to work; we've got lots to do in only 90 minutes," said Benedict Showalter, board chair, kicking off the monthly meeting of the governance committee of the

Metro Transit board of directors. "What's your committee cooked up for next month's board agenda, Barbara?" Benedict asked, turning to the chair of the board's external relations committee, Barbara Munson. "Well, we've got some really interesting and important items this time around," Barbara responded. "First, the committee has augmented and polished the image statement that we brainstormed at our strategic planning retreat last month, defining how Metro Transit needs to be seen by the public-at-large and our key stakeholders, and we're ready to run it by the board. Assuming we have some discussion, I think we'll probably need twenty minutes max for that item. We'll factor in the input we get and run the statement by the board one last time at the meeting after next.

"The committee has also analyzed the information from the customer survey that our PR firm conducted, and we've come up with a list of what appear to be the most serious gaps between particular elements of our image statement and customer perceptions documented in the survey," Barbara went on. "We want to run over these image issues at the board meeting, and make our board colleagues aware that the public relations operating plan and budget that staff are working on will focus on addressing the issues." "Does the external relations committee have any action items to introduce at the board meeting, Barbara?" Benedict asked. "Yes, we'll be proposing that the board pass a resolution adopting our recommended position on the public transportation funding bill that's now before the State Senate. All in all, I'm estimating that we'll need around 45 minutes at the board meeting, certainly no more, to get through our agenda."

"Thanks, Barbara. Now what about the performance monitoring and audit committee?" Benedict asked, turning to the chair, Bart Wohlstein. "The financial report is pretty routine, so we'll go through it pretty quickly, and I don't expect many, if any, questions," Bart said, "but we should probably block out a full half-hour for presentation and discussion of our proposed new financial management policy, recommending that Cathy [the CEO] be authorized to sign contracts that are in the budget for any amount up to a maximum of $50,000, without the treasurer having to co-sign."

"How do you think board members will react to the policy, Bart?" asked Sherry Gerulitis, chair of the planning committee. "Well, Sherry, I think if we pushed the board to make a decision at the meeting, they'd adopt the policy by a slim majority, but we'd have some pretty upset board members." "I think it would be really unwise to press the board on this one, Bart," Benedict said, "and since time isn't of essence on this one, I recommend that we stage discussion of the policy as a special half-hour work session at the board meeting, making clear that we want to explore the pros and cons thoroughly and give all board members ample opportunity to raise questions." "I agree," responded Bart, "and I know the committee will concur. We'll plan on bringing the policy to the board for action at the September meeting, at the earliest."

The governance committee spent fifteen minutes or so reviewing agenda items coming from Sherry's planning committee agenda, after which they reached consensus on steps they would take to deal with lagging attendance at planning committee meetings, including calling three board members whose attendance had been erratic. They then spent a few minutes deciding how to re-structure the public comment section of the board agenda, and approved the CEO's recommended schedule for holding the first four board meetings next year in various locations around the metropolitan area, after which the meeting was adjourned.

This isn't an extraordinary example. Increasingly numbers of nonprofit and public boards are using their governance or board operations committee as a very effective vehicle for coordinating and managing their boards' operations. Of course, the CEO is always at the table, and active board involvement in managing its own affairs as a governing body isn't ever at the expense of the CEO, who, as an integral member of the Strategic Governing Team, makes sure that the process is well-supported and plays an active role in the committee's deliberations. The old fashioned approach of the CEO's merely developing the board agenda and running it by the board chair misses an important opportunity to build board ownership and accountability.

BOARD HUMAN RESOURCE DEVELOPMENT

Like all other organizations, boards are essentially people, and one of the important ways to develop your board's governing capacity—along with designing structure and process—is to develop the people on your board. Developing your board as a human resource basically involves your governance or board operations committee in: (1) developing the composition of the board; and (2) developing board member governing knowledge and skills.

Nonprofit and public boards fill vacancies in various ways. The great majority of nonprofit boards at the local level are self-appointing, but the members of many public transportation boards are appointed by mayors and county chief executives, school boards are for the most part elected by voters living in the school district, and association board members are typically elected by the association's members. No matter how the members of your board are chosen, you can influence the filling of vacancies in order to strengthen your board's composition. The first step is for your governance or board operations committee to fashion a two-tiered profile of the ideal board you're looking for over the long run:

1. The broad categories of people you'd like to see on the board (for example: representatives of the business commu-

nity; minorities; women; representatives of key stakeholder organizations)

2. The more specific attributes and qualifications you're looking for in individual board members, regardless of the category they fall into (for example: having the time to commit to the work of the board; having contacts in the community).

The second step is for your governance or board operations committee to develop and execute a strategy for filling vacancies with people who fit the profile. For self-appointing boards, the strategy can be quite direct (identify the people and go get them), but for elected boards and boards selected by third parties such as the mayor or county CEO, the strategy will necessarily be less direct—aimed at influencing voters and appointing authorities.

REAL-LIFE EXAMPLES

Let's look at some real-life examples of boards that have creatively shaped their composition in the interest of higher-impact governing:

- **Enriching the Mix**
  The governance committee of a self-appointing nursing home board I worked with not too long ago decided that it needed to diversify the mix of people on the board by consciously recruiting women, small business owners, hospital executives, and representatives of the rapidly growing Latino community. The members of the governance committee didn't set specific targets, but agreed that in identifying candidates to fill vacancies, they would pay special attention to these under-represented categories.

- **Employing a Profile**
  The executive committee of a public transportation system in the southwestern US provided the appointing

64

authorities with a profile of attributes and qualifications they were looking for in board members, and asked that the profile at least be considered in filling board vacancies. The list included: "knowledgeable about transportation issues;" "able to commit the time to committee and full board meetings;" "experience on at least two other public or nonprofit boards;" "demonstrated interpersonal skills;" and the like.

- **Adding "Outside" Directors**
The board operations committee of a state association whose members are insurance agents recommended that the board amend the bylaws to allow three of the fifteen seats on the board to be filled by "outside" board members who aren't insurance agents, as a means both to enrich board deliberations and to build ties with important stakeholder organizations in the state. The amendment, which was adopted, provided that the three outside seats would be filled by the board itself, while the other twelve seats would be filled by members voting at the annual meeting.

- **Running a "Farm System"**
The governance committee of the elected board of an international trade association has put in place a kind of "farm system" for identifying candidates to stand for election to the board. The chairs of the association's several technical advisory committees consisting of non-board volunteers (for example, professional development, annual conference program, and certification committees) are provided with the profile of desirable board member attributes and qualifications and asked to identify committee members closely fitting the profile and provide their names to the governance committee. The committee takes its nominating committee role so seriously that committee members actually check references and the top

65

candidates being considered are interviewed, in person if possible but at least by phone.

DEVELOPING GOVERNING KNOWLEDGE AND SKILLS

In my interviews with thousands of board members over the years, I've heard this lament countless times: "I spent my first year or so on the board just learning the ropes—listening, observing, and keeping my mouth shut most of the time. Talk about on-the-job learning! I can't recall anyone ever telling me exactly what I was supposed to be doing as a board member, although I heard a lot about the agency's mission, programs and budget from the executive director in what I guess was my orientation session the week before my first board meeting." Isn't it ironic—when you consider the complex, demanding, and high-stakes governing work that boards do—that many if not most nonprofit and public organizations invest a fair amount of time and money in staff development, but few in my experience invest much in developing board member governing knowledge and skills? So the average new board member not only doesn't hit the ground running, he or she is more likely to be struggling to stay upright. This is totally unnecessary and inexcusable— and easily corrected.

A growing number of nonprofit and public boards these days are paying much closer attention to the development of board members by adopting an annual plan and budget for board member development. For example, the governance committee of a school board in a rapidly growing district oversees a program consisting of the following elements:

- **Orienting New Board Members**
  New board members are provided with a formal orientation conducted by members of the governance committee, who concentrate on the work of the board, going over: the board's governing mission; the committee structure; the section of the bylaws relating to the board;

the board member performance targets and standards; and the like. Incoming board members also receive a thorough briefing from the superintendent on the district's vision, mission, educational programs, and budget, but the focus of orientation is the board itself.

- **Assigning Mentors**
New board members are also linked up with a longer-tenured board member, who serves for the first year as a mentor, checking in with the new board member periodically to discuss how things are going, answer questions, and share tricks of the governing trade.

- **Running a Lending Library**
The board development budget covers the purchase of books on nonprofit and public governance for board members, and the CEO's executive assistant is responsible for scanning certain publications and circulating pertinent articles on governance matters among board members.

- **Providing Continuing Education**
And the budget also covers continuing education for board members in the rapidly developing field of nonprofit and public governance, which has up to now consisted of an annual governance workshop conducted at headquarters and the opportunity to attend the annual conference of the American Association of School Administrators and the National School Boards Association every three years.

BOARD PERFORMANCE MANAGEMENT
The great majority of board members I've observed and worked with over the years have welcomed having their boards'—and their individual—governing performance assessed. That's not surprising, when you consider that the kind of successful and high-achieving people who populate boards are very familiar

with setting goals and measuring performance as a powerful tool for advancement. In fact, I've found that nothing tends to offend and erode the enthusiasm and commitment of really productive board members faster than knowing that colleagues on their board can get away with sub-par governing performance because no one's paying attention to board performance management. Indeed, in my experience if a nonprofit or public board takes the trouble to regularly and systematically assess its governing performance and take action to correct problems, that board will be a magnet to attract high-quality candidates.

As is true of all other governing functions, if you want board performance management to be capably handled, the function needs a committee home. Your board governance or board operations committee obviously fits the bill, for two reasons: it's accountable for board operations, and it consists of the board's leadership, particularly the chairs of its governing engines, the standing committees.

The first step in building your board performance management program is to establish targets—for the board as a whole and for individual board members. Your board's standing committees are ideal vehicles for establishing concrete governing targets for the board as a whole, and you'll want the governance or board operations committee to annually review and reach agreement on each committee's proposed targets. For example, the planning committee might be committed to updating your organization's values and vision statements over the coming year; the performance monitoring committee might set as one of its goals revamping the external auditor selection process; or the community relations committee might promise to get the long-discussed board member speakers bureau going.

Your governance or board operations committee can also fashion and keep updated a set of targets relating to individual board member behavior, for example: attending committee and full board meetings; participating in important organizational events, such as the annual dinner; speaking on behalf of the organization in appropriate forums; abiding by conflict of interest rules; not giving direction to staff members; and the like.

It makes sense for the governance or board operations committee to take a management-by-exception approach to individual board member performance: looking primarily to committee chairs to alert the group to individual performance problems and dealing with them as they're red-flagged (almost always by a counseling call). Only in extreme cases of dereliction of duty would formal action, such as asking for a board member's resignation, be merited. As far as overall board performance is concerned, one approach that I've seen work quite effectively is for the governance or board operations committee to hold a governing report card session early in the new year, at which committee chairs report on progress in achieving their targets over the past year and agreement is reached on the targets for the new year.

Experience has taught me that you should avoid elaborate self-assessment questionnaires and checklists, primarily because they tend to direct attention to minor details at the expense of serious governing issues. Using your standing committees as the vehicle for setting and measuring performance is far more effective, assuming that your board has a well-designed structure.

6. CEO AND EXECUTIVE TEAM SUPPORT

FOCUSING ON COMMITTEES

As you know, governing is a true team sport. No matter how qualified, dedicated, and committed your board members are, they can't carry the governing ball alone. High-impact governing depends on strong, continuous CEO and executive team support. There's no point in my wasting your precious time by repeating the conventional little golden rules of staffing a board, such as getting the board meeting packet to board members well in advance; you know them inside-out. Instead, my aim in this concluding chapter is to describe the kind of executive support structure and process you've got to put in place to ensure that your board's standing committees fulfill their tremendous promise as "governing engines":

> • Ensuring that the decisions and judgments making up the bread and butter work of governing are made in a full and timely fashion, and

> • Serving as vehicles for committee members and the CEO to map out detailed processes for involving board members in key governing streams, such as planning and performance monitoring.

I don't really have any choice but to focus on standing committees in this concluding chapter since your board won't travel very far on the journey toward high-impact governing unless its committees are firmly established and fully functional. Of course, I'm not talking about just any committees—and certainly not old-time silo committees—but a contemporary structure of standing committees that are organized around the actual flows of governing judgments and decisions, as I describe in Chapter 3.

A DAUNTING CHALLENGE EARLY-ON

The executive support structure and process I'll be describing is essential to ensure that your board's standing committees function effectively, but it's especially important when you're getting new committees up and running. A new committee structure tends to be highly fragile in its infancy, and there is always a clear and present danger that things will fall apart, for three major reasons:

1. **The majority of your board members are unlikely to have a firm grasp of the functional division of labor among the new committees,** and their ownership of the new structure will be minimal early in the implementation process. Being experienced and successful business people and professionals, they will naturally hedge their bets until they've seen the new committees function reasonably well.

2. **Your new committee structure will be going against the current during the implementation process.** Having to participate in an unfamiliar structure will early-on feel extremely uncomfortable to many if not most board members, and some might even worry (perhaps unconsciously) about their ability to perform in the new structure. Discomfort and fear of failure are, as you know, classic enemies of commitment and a primary cause of inertia.

3. **And you are likely to have to contend with the centrifugal force generated by your new committee chairs**—typically Type-As who naturally expect to produce immediate results and make a real difference. It is always wise to keep in mind that the take-command types serving on boards aren't inclined to sit back and patiently wait to be instructed on their appropriate roles. If they sense a vacuum, they will naturally fill it. There is always a very real danger that committee chairs will charge ahead in fashioning their own agendas, outstripping staff and throwing them on the defensive. Once a committee has gotten off on the wrong foot, you have a serous political—not simply technical—problem on

your hands: trying to get board members to backtrack and start over in the right direction.

A MODEL EXECUTIVE SUPPORT STRUCTURE

You can think of your executive support structure as a special-purpose organization within your wider nonprofit or public organization, whose express purpose is managing the process of developing agendas and materials for meetings of the standing committees and full board, ensuring that:

- Committees are engaged in interesting and productive work for which committee members feel ownership.

- Committee chairs are well-prepared to lead meetings.

- Quality control is rigorously maintained in the development of agendas and other documentation for committee meetings.

I'll be describing the elements of a model support structure that has been thoroughly tested in practice, but I know some readers work in smaller organizations that have neither the time nor staff to implement the support structure in its full glory. But the closer you can come to building the following elements into your own support structure, the more favorable the odds will be that your board's standing committees will function effectively:

- The CEO's Governance Chief of Staff
- The standing committee Chief Staff Liaisons
- The Chief Staff Liaison Working Group
- The executive team sitting as the Governance Steering Committee

Governance Chief of Staff

The Governance Chief of Staff—designated by the CEO to head what you might call the CEO's "Board Office"— has overall responsibility for making sure that the support structure functions as intended: scheduling key meetings (for example, of the Chief Staff Liaison Working Group), monitoring quality control, preparing for—and following up on—governance or board operations committee meetings, and overseeing preparation of the board meeting packet. The Governance Chief of Staff should be a full-fledged member of the executive team who has easy access to the CEO and shares the CEO's commitment to a high-impact governing board.

Chief Staff Liaisons

The Chief Staff Liaisons are members of the executive team assigned by the CEO to work with each of the standing committees. In a nutshell the Chief Staff Liaison for a particular committee is accountable three ways for his or her committee's performance as a "governing engine": (1) to the CEO; (2) to the committee chair; and (3) to his or her colleagues on the executive team. The detailed responsibilities of the Chief Staff Liaison include:

> • Planning future committee agendas, relating to the dual roles of each committee: (1) preparing for regular board business meetings; (2) designing processes for Board member involvement in the governing functions of each committee

> • Reviewing future agendas with the Chief Staff Liaison Working Group, the executive team sitting as the Governance Steering Committee, and his or her committee chair

> • Ensuring that his or her committee chair is well-prepared to lead committee deliberations

• Overseeing the preparation of written material and oral briefings for committee meetings, in this capacity exercising rigorous quality control and making sure that written materials are transmitted well in advance of committee meetings

• Preparing the committee report to the board for regular business meetings and making sure that the committee chair is prepared to present the report and to answer questions that might come up in the board meeting

• Participating in the regular meetings of the Chief Staff Liaison Working Group

• Preparing for a regularly scheduled executive team session dedicated to supporting the board and its standing committees that the CEO should convene at least monthly. The Chief Staff Liaison is responsible for leading discussion of upcoming committee agendas at these meetings and for facilitating agreement on staff responsibilities for preparing material for upcoming committee meetings.

Chief Staff Liaison Working Group

The Chief Staff Liaison Working Group—convened by the Governance Chief of Staff and consisting of the Chief Staff Liaisons—meets regularly to discuss preparation for standing committee meetings. These informal sessions will normally focus on upcoming committee agenda items, special staff preparation time required to deal with particular items, and problems that need to be resolved.

Governance Steering Committee

The executive team meets regularly (typically monthly) as the Governance Steering Committee. Chaired by the CEO and led by the Chief Staff Liaisons, the Governance Steering Committee meeting is where standing committee agenda items are thoroughly reviewed and finalized for review with the committee chairs. It is also where agreement is reached on allocating staff time to governance matters. For example, the Chief Staff Liaison to the board's planning committee might need support from his or her executive team colleagues in preparing an environmental scan for the upcoming board strategic planning work session being hosted by the committee.

THE COMMITTEE AGENDA DEVELOPMENT PROCESS
The following steps are intended to ensure thorough preparation for standing committee meetings:

• Chief Staff Liaisons give serious thought to future agenda items for their respective committees, projecting as far into the future as feasible, along the two main streams of committee activity: (1) the flow of action and information items to regular board business meetings; and (2) the design of processes for board involvement in such governing functions as strategic planning and performance monitoring.

• The Chief Staff Liaison Working Group meets to discuss and reach agreement on agendas for upcoming standing committee meetings.

• The Chief Staff Liaisons review these agendas with the whole executive team in a regularly scheduled meeting that is chaired by the CEO and dedicated to governance matters.

• The Chief Staff Liaisons then review the agendas with their standing committee chairs, securing their buy-in and making sure they understand each item on the agenda. Note: Although committee chairs might occasionally be the original source of agenda items, as a regular practice this would be chaotic, potentially threatening the integrity of the committee structure.

• Once the chairs have signed off on the committee agendas, the Chief Staff Liaisons coordinate the preparation of material for the upcoming committee meetings, ensuring that a complete, high-quality packet is ready to send to the committees well in advance of their regular meetings. It is recommended that the transmittal of all agenda material to the standing committees be handled by the Governance Chief of Staff.

• It is critical that the Chief Staff Liaisons meet (typically via phone) with their respective standing committee chairs to go over the agenda items with the proverbial "fine-tooth comb," making sure that the chairs are well-prepared to present the committee's report to the board governance or operations committee and ultimately the full board at its regular business meeting.

• It makes sense for the Chief Staff Liaisons to be responsible for writing the reports of their committees to the board, employing a standard format that the CEO and Governance Steering Committee adopt. You definitely will not want formal, legalistic minutes of the "he said/she said" variety. Instead, I suggest a summary of main points memorandum that is divided into for-information and for-action sections, referring in the case of for-action items to the specific location in the board packet that goes out for regular business meetings.

• The board governance or operations committee meets to finalize the board agenda, based on the recommendations of the other three standing committees. Of course, the CEO will propose the agenda, rather than it's actually being constructed at the meeting. The governance or board operations committee also reaches agreement on the approximate allocation of time to each standing committee's items, depending on each committee's action and information items being sent to the board. The Chief Staff Liaisons should always participate in these meetings, along with the Governance Chief of Staff and, of course, the CEO.

• As appropriate, the Chief Staff Liaisons meet with their respective committee chairs again before the board meeting to go over the content of committee reports, making sure the chairs are well-prepared to present their action and informational items at the board meeting.

PREPARING BOARD MEMBERS TO PARTICIPATE

Putting a well-designed executive support structure and process in place is a critical step in implementing your board's new standing committee structure, but you also want to be sure that all board members understand the roles and functions of the new committees before they begin participating in the structure. One tried and true way to ensure that they're sufficiently knowledgeable is to hold a special orientation session at one of your board meetings, consisting of three key agenda items:

1. The board chair presents an overview, which might include the genesis of the new committee structure and review of the board's Governing Mission.

2. Committee chairs present the detailed functional descriptions of each of their committees, employing PowerPoint slides, and respond to questions about the functional division of labor among the committees.

3. The board chair reviews the committee operating guidelines and addresses questions.

Chief Staff Liaisons should make sure that their respective committee chairs are well-prepared to present the PowerPoint descriptions of their committees and to address any questions that come up. If a committee chair is obviously unclear about the functional division of labor, or is easily stumped by questions, then the whole structure will lose credibility in the eyes of other board members. Therefore, preparation for this orientation session is a high-stakes matter. Accordingly, if at all possible a "dress rehearsal" involving the board chair, committee chairs, the CEO, and Chief Staff Liaisons should be held, at which the presenters can run through their presentations, questions can be anticipated, and possible responses can be discussed.

IN CLOSING: GO FOR IT!

Public and nonprofit organizations around the country spend hundreds of millions of dollars providing essential services in diverse areas, such as education, health care, aging, social services, economic and community development, and transportation. Our society's well-being heavily depends on the effectiveness and efficiency of these organizations, which in turn depend on the leadership of governing bodies that do truly high-impact governing work in close partnership with their CEO. Your organization's well-being depends as well on strong board leadership and a solid board-CEO partnership. The stakes are tremendous, and we really can't afford to have underperforming boards and dysfunctional board-CEO partnerships.

You can put the High-Impact Governing Model™ that I've described in this book to work in your organization as a powerful, well-tested vehicle for developing the kind of high-impact governing body and solid board-CEO partnership that these changing, challenging times demand. You'll have to spend some time and money, but you'll be making a wise investment that will yield a rich return, in terms not only of a secure and flourishing organization, but also satisfied, committed board members and a really solid board-CEO partnership that can stand the test of challenging times. Don't wait. Just go for it and put the High-Impact Governing Model™ to work in your organization.

ABOUT THE AUTHOR

Doug Eadie is the founder and president of Doug Eadie & Company, a firm that specializes in building governing board leadership capacity and strengthening the board-CEO partnership. Over the past twenty-five years, Doug has worked with more than 500 public and nonprofit organizations.

He is the author of sixteen other books on nonprofit leadership, including *High-Impact Governing in a Nutshell* and *Extraordinary Board Leadership*. Before founding his consulting practice, Doug held several senior positions in the public and nonprofit sectors. He is a Phi Beta Kappa graduate of the University of Illinois at Urbana and received his master of science in management degree from the Weatherhead School at Case Western Reserve University.

OTHER BOOKS BY DOUG EADIE

The Board-Savvy Superintendent (with Paul Houston). Roman & Littlefield Education, Lanham, Maryland, 2002.

Boards That Work. ASAE, Washington, DC, 1994.

Changing By Design. Jossey-Bass, San Francisco, 1997.

Eight Keys to an Extraordinary Board-Superintendent Partnership. Roman & Littlefield Education, Lanham, Maryland, 2003.

Extraordinary Board Leadership. Jones and Bartlett, Sudbury, Massachusetts, 2001.

The Extraordinary CEO. ASAE, Washington, DC, 1999.

The Extraordinary CEO in Public Transportation. APTA, Washington, DC, 2000.

Five Habits of High-Impact School Boards. Roman & Little-field Education, Lanhan, Maryland, 2005.

High-Impact Governing in a Nutshell. ASAE, Washington, DC, 2004.

Visit www.DougEadie.com for more information on books, CDs, and web-based training from Doug Eadie & Company.